TEXACO
COLLECTIBLES

Robert W.D. Ball

with
Price Guide

Schiffer Publishing Ltd

77 Lower Valley Road, Atglen, PA 19310

DEDICATION

I am of an age where I delight in the fact that I have a teen-age grandson. I also delight in the fact that I do not have to raise him and go through all the agonies, and joys, that this age period bestows upon one and all! Aaron has grown up seeing cars re-built in the garage, modified and enhanced as the case may be, and as a result, has more than a whiff of oil and gas in his blood.

With the hope that this book may mean something special to him, as he is special to his Grandfather, I dedicate this book to Aaron Henninger of Wadsworth, Ohio.

Copyright 1994 by Robert W.D. Ball.
Library of Congress Number: 94-65613

Printed in Hong Kong.
ISBN: 0-88740-656-4

Published by Schiffer Publishing, Ltd.
77 Lower Valley Road
Atglen, PA 19310
Please write for a free catalog.
This book may be purchased from the publisher.
Please include $2.95 postage.
Try your bookstore first.

We are interested in hearing from authors
with book ideas on related subjects.

Title page photo:
Wilshire Boulevard, Los Angeles, c. 1928. Note the exquisitely dressed station attendant in white uniform, right down to polished puttees and shoes. The station is highlighted by the filigree iron work around both entrances.
Courtesy of the Texaco Corporation

Where it all started! A view of the Wupperfeld Texaco station on "Gasoline Alley," U.S. #1, the Post Road in Stratford, Connecticut, C. 1936

Acknowledgements

In the early 1930s, Joseph Wupperfeld passed his state boards for CPA, found work as an accountant, and hated it! Shortly after giving up his truncated career as an accountant, he was able to obtain a Texaco gas station in Greenwich, Connecticut; soon thereafter, he made a move to Stratford, Connecticut and began to build his career in the retail gas business.

Young Joe, his son, managed to spend lots of time at the station, growing up with grease and oil under his nails and the smell of gasoline in his nostrils...he never forgot it, and got his first nudge into the collecting of Texaco gas station memorabilia. Memories are still fresh of the drive-on grease pit, with his Dad in bow tie and peaked cap going down to service a LaSalle or Pierce Arrow. He can almost see the men that used to hang around in the small office talking cars and motorcycles, watching the cars that came in to fill up for a few dollars, while the attendants made sure that the oil was checked and the windshield was clean.

His father has been long gone, but as a result of those days, Joe has amassed a wonderful collection of Texaco-related items that are being shown for the first time in this book. Here, you will find early examples of the various oil and related products cans in use, promotional items sold or given away by the individual stations; metal, paper and plastic signs, Texaco toys, as well as a myriad of other related items. Joe is extremely broad in his areas of collecting, with a house that is a veritable museum of different interests, ranging from Fire Fighting collectibles, to everything that was done on Prince Valiant of the comics! When Joe goes, it will be with a smile on his face, for he will truly have had all the toys!

My deep thanks also go to the Texaco Corporation for their ready willingness to share the contents of their historical archives with an author hungry for authentic background material. Cherie Voris, Company Archivist, extended herself far beyond what anyone could reasonably expect, and did it with the utmost thoughtfulness. Thanks also to Terry Fisher, Editor of the "Marketer" for his insightful critique of this project.

Introduction

This is a book, not about Texaco the company, but Texaco, the source of gas station collectibles. It is important in the overall view of this book, however, to also know some of the background of one of the largest oil and gasoline related companies in the history of the United States.

Amid scenes reminiscent of the gold-rush days of California and the Klondike, the Lucas gusher at Spindletop in 1901 created an oil boom in Texas that brought about the small predecessor of the Texas Company. Two men, Joseph Stephen Cullinan and Arnold Schlaet, through their sagacity and energy, founded the company and held it together, while all around them their rivals succumbed to failure. Putting together more capital, Cullinan and Schlaet formed an even larger company, The Texas Company, on April 7, 1902. It not only survived but thrived.

Cullinan had started at the bottom in the oilfields of Pennsylvania and survived as a giant among the pioneers of the petroleum industry in the Southwest. With an entrepreneurial talent in finance and sales, the German-born Schlaet's initial interest in the oil business was as an investor. Thus, the prime players of the Texas Company merged, each complementing the other, with Schlaet securing the funds that enabled Cullinan to "do the job."

The Company's first year proved to be a big one. The new company contracted for a million barrels of oil, bought the equipment to handle it, secured the markets, took a profitable gamble at Sour Lake, Texas, and declared its first dividend!

In 1905, the Company was a major player in all the great Southwest oil strikes ... at the same time establishing their first overseas marketing enterprises in Antwerp, Belgium. In 1907, the Delaware River Terminal was opened to bring Texaco products to the East coast. Texaco's first registered trademark, the red star with the green "T" superimposed, appeared that year. In 1909 Texaco began the production of oil cans at Port Arthur, Texas. This was also the year that the Texas Company recognized the new and rapidly growing market in gasoline for automobiles. It produced what it called "No.4 Motor Gasoline" at its West Dallas refinery, once again demonstrating that Texaco was a prime force in shaping the future of the oil industry.

Initially, the motorist filled his tank by means of a can and funnel, being careful to strain the gas through a chamois cloth in order to remove foreign matter and dirt, which, at that time, often contaminated the product. With improvement in the quality of the gasoline came improvement in the means of getting it into the tank. Before long, a motorist was able to drive into a garage and have an attendant fill the tank from a barrel equipped with a hand pump and hose. Then, with the introduction of underground storage tanks in 1910, the day of the curbstone pump had arrived! Very quickly, the filling station and the ubiquitous gasoline pump became familiar to the American public. 1913 saw the advent of the first Texaco service stations and in 1915 the Company introduced uniform hanging signs.

The overseas markets, in the meantime, had not been overlooked, with the tanker "Texas," the largest ever built at that time, going into regular service between Port Arthur and continental ports. This was the start of the tanker fleet.

With a continuing program of expansion, 1911 saw the opening of the Texas Company's fifth refinery in Lockport, Illinois. An era ended when Cullinan, who perhaps had done more than any other to create the Texas Company, resigned in 1913 at the insistence of the board of directors. World War One brought an immense increase in the need for petroleum products, while during this same era, the automobile become a necessity for much of the American public.

Due to the phenomenal increase in the use of the automobile, by 1920, Texaco's assets had quadrupled. Texaco made a specialty of automobile gasoline and lubricating oils, laying the foundation for leadership in service to the motorist that remains unsurpassed to the present day. In 1921, Texaco introduced the Easy Pour two-quart oil can, possibly the first commercial oil can! 1922 saw the Texaco Company advertising nationally, while standard service station design was introduced nationwide in 1923. By 1928, Texaco became the first oil company to market its product in all 48 states.

"Fire Chief" gasoline came on the market in 1932, eventually becoming synonymous with the name of Ed Wynn, a wonderful comedic actor of the 1930s. 1935 found distinctive, custom-designed streamlined gas tank trucks making deliveries to all the Texaco service stations nation-wide. 1938 welcomed "Sky Chief" gasoline to the market, and two years later, Texaco began its long sponsorship of the Metropolitan Opera radio program. In 1948, an early entry into television, the "Texaco Star Theater," featuring the multi-talented Milton Berle, became a staple of household viewing. In fact, on show nights, the normal household events almost ground to a halt while families across the United States huddled around their television screens and shared in the hilarious antics of "Uncle Miltie"!

With assets topping $1 billion in 1947, the Company opened New Jersey's Eagle Point refinery in 1949, the first to handle imported oil on the East Coast. The growing importance of imported oil led to the opening of the 1,068 mile long pipeline system carrying crude oil from the Abqaiq field in Saudi Arabia to the Mediterranean Sea in 1950. 1955 heralded the introduction of a new, all-temperature oil, Advanced Custom Made Havoline. Adding to its assets, Texaco acquired Seaboard Oil Company in

Newark, New Jersey garage filling station, c.1913.
Courtesy of the Texaco Corporation

1958, Paragon Oil Company on the East Coast in 1959, the TXL Oil Corporation in 1962, and Deutsche Erdol A.G. of West Germany in 1966.

Getting a jump on the competition, Texaco introduced lead-free gasoline in 1970. The decade of the 1970s was a decade of dramatic change for both the energy industry and the customers it served. The rising costs of petroleum products spurred greater conservation efforts, reduced energy demand, and encouraged the search for alternative energy sources. By early 1974, many countries had begun to take steps to lessen consumption, with resulting hardships to consumers. During this decade, Texaco undertook tremendous capital investments in order to expand and develop its worldwide integrated enterprise. Improved products were reflected in the new "Havoline Supreme Motor Oil" in 1979.

In the 1980s, Texaco began closing inefficient operations, while at the same time upgrading and investing in the profitable sectors of its operations. 1981 saw the ap-

pearance of the latest Texaco logo...a red T placed inside a white star and a red circle, all placed on a black background. This marked the introduction of Texaco's "System 2000" stations. Some of the most important steps taken by Texaco in the 1980s involved a series of acquisitions, including the purchase of Getty Oil Company in 1984, which was later challenged in court by Pennzoil Company. This was settled in 1987, and from that point, Texaco moved aggressively forward with its restructuring plans.

We now come to Texaco today. Presently Texaco is engaged directly or indirectly in all phases of the petroleum industry in almost every part of the world. It is ranked by *Fortune Magazine* as one of the top 10 revenue producing companies with approximately $42 billion in annual sales. Due to its constant attention to detail and forward planning, Texaco should finish the 1990s as a giant in the petroleum industry, moving aggressively forward into the 21st Century while maintaining its leadership.

Contents

A curb-side filling station in New Orleans, Louisiana, c. 1915.
These store front stations replaced old-time livery stables and
garages where gasoline had been sold up to that time.
Courtesy of the Texaco Corporation

Hartford, Connecticut curb side service station, c. 1916.
Courtesy of the Texaco Corporation

Texaco curbside filling station, Baton Rouge, Louisiana, c. 1922.
Courtesy of the Texaco Corporation

A typical early 1940s Texaco station, ready to handle all of your automotive needs, from gas, to new tires, to a car wash!

A typical 1930s Texaco outhouse, which has been converted to a hobby gas station by the collector.

A side view of the former outhouse, showing a large Texaco sign from a station standard.

Texaco Gas Station Equipment and Products Containers

Collector interest in Texaco spans an eclectic variety of items. Foremost among them are the various pieces of equipment without which no service station can operate. To be lucky (and persistent enough) to acquire an original early visible gas pump or a portable bulk oil dispenser is the delight of the collector. The early oil containers first introduced in the early 1920s are always prime targets, as are their modern day successors.

Aside from attending collectors' meets, where there is generally frenzied buying, selling, and swapping, traveling those back roads in search of old, long established gas stations has paid dividends for many collectors and added to the "thrill of the hunt." Tucked away in storage areas, in overhead beams, in back lot sheds, the persistent hunter may find salvageable pieces of equipment, globes, and sundry containers that the owner is willing to part with very reasonably, just to do a little "housecleaning."

I think back to a time about fifty years ago when some fellows I knew were putting themselves through college by digging in an old dump area that had seen continuous use from the late 1700s. These unpolished entrepreneurs were enjoying remarkable success from the salvaging and sale of the old bottles they unearthed, some from the colonial days, and each of them netted out about $4,000-5,000 for a summer's digging. One of these fellows was so attracted to the other things he uncovered in his search for bottles that he started his own collection of early oil containers, both metal and glass...the collection of quality pieces from these diggings was truly amazing!

1926 Texaco pump, hand cranked.
Courtesy of the Texaco Corporation

Texaco 10-gallon visible pumps, c. 1925.
Courtesy of the Texaco Corporation

Clock face pumps at a Fort Wayne, Indiana Texaco service station.
Courtesy of the Texaco Corporation

Tokheim dial pumps, c. 1930s.
Courtesy of the Texaco Corporation

Texaco Fire Chief and Sky Chief pumps, c. 1940s.
Courtesy of the Texaco Corporation

A beautifully preserved 1938 clock-face pump

A visible pump, presently in use as a decorator item at a North Carolina Texaco station.

Updated Sky Chief pump; note the indicated price of gas! Oh, for the good old days!
Courtesy of the Texaco Corporation

A 1940s bulk oil dispenser in wonderful, unrestored condition.

A foam fire extinguisher, a 1940s fixture at pump stations and airports in unrestored condition.

The "New System 3" Texaco combination pump system.
Courtesy of the Texaco Corporation

The updated version of the Fire Chief pump.
Courtesy of the Texaco Corporation

From the 1930s, a gas station parts cleaning container with an interior circulating pump.

Thin "T" Texaco pump globe from the 1960s.

Cover from the February, 1916 Texaco Star magazine.
Courtesy of the Texaco Corporation

Fat "T" Texaco pump globe replacement lens.

Texaco Promotional Materials and Station Accessories

Early on, Texaco learned the value of promotional marketing. Studies have shown that adults who identified with a product as a child continued to identify into adulthood, becoming part of a "permanent" market base.

With the proliferation of service stations across the United States after World War One, competition increased between the major suppliers. Marketing and promotions became a way of life for the individual service station, with banners, signs and give-aways of every imaginable description. In order to build a loyal following, Texaco, like many other companies, appealed to the father through the child. Models of all manner of Texaco equipment were to be found at the local Texaco station, from tank trucks to fire engines and ship models that attracted both youngsters and the "kid" still lurking inside the father. With fill-ups, mugs emblazoned with the Texaco logo were given as premiums along with key chains, bottle openers, ash trays, model banks and a myriad of other products. Success breeds success, and this type of product identification was no exception...the idea continues to this day!

On the following pages are found a wide variety of the marketing tools that Texaco employed over the years. Some are more common that others, but in the long run, they all combine to illustrate the tremendous appeal and success to be found in the marketing history of one of the largest fuel producing companies in the United States.

Sterling silver numbered "Port Arthur Works" employee badge.

Obverse and reverse of rare key chain tag with the early Texaco mascot "Scotties," c. 1930s

Texaco's first service station in Houston, Texas was located at 706 San Jacinto, c. 1917.
Courtesy of the Texaco Corporation

Full-time service station salesman's winter uniform, c. 1972.
Courtesy of the Texaco Corporation

Full-time service station salesman's summer uniform, c. 1972.
Courtesy of the Texaco Corporation

Full-time service station salesman's winter uniform, including jacket, c. 1972.
Courtesy of the Texaco Corporation

Part-time service station salesman's winter uniform, c. 1972.
Courtesy of the Texaco Corporation

Part-time service station salesman's summer uniform, c. 1972.
Courtesy of the Texaco Corporation

Texaco Service Station salesman's uniform logos, c. 1972.
Courtesy of the Texaco Corporation

Grouping showing Texaco uniform jacket, pants, shirts, ties and hats, c. 1972.
Courtesy of the Texaco Corporation

Texaco jacket patch.

A great grouping of Texaco uniform shirts, tie and hat from the 70s. If these are found in this condition today, they command premium prices from collectors.
Courtesy of the Texaco Corporation

Announcing
THE NEW MIRACLE BLEND
ENDUROWEAVE
DACRON GABARDINE
AT NEW LOWER PRICES

E ndurance PLUS
N icer Appearing
D acron/Rayon Gabardine
U nsurpassed Quality
R esists Stains, Wrinkles, Shrinking and Fading
O utwears Cotton by 300%
W ash & Wearable . . . Dries Wrinkle Free
E asy to Care For
A cid-Proof
V aluable Savings
E xceptional Strength and Durability

JACKET
This is your smartly styled Eisenhower Jacket (Stock No. 1743) made of Unitog's new miracle blend fabric EnDuroWeave Dacron/Rayon Gabardine. This Acid-Proof jacket has reinforced elbows, double button cuffs, an adjustable waistband, and a full zipper closure. It is double stitched and heavily bartacked at all points of strain to give greater strength and durability. For those real cold winter days ahead this forestry green jacket is equipped with a half track for either the vest style zip-in zip-out dacron liner (Stock No. 100-VL) or the long sleeve style (Stock No. 200-SL).
ENDUROWEAVE DACRON/RAYON GABARDINE JACKET
STOCK NO. 1743..ONLY $8.95

TROUSERS
These winterweight EnDuroWeave Dacron/Rayon Gabardine Trousers (Stock No. 1643) will give you maximum protection from cold and wind this winter. These forestry green trousers feature double lined pockets, double stitching and bartacking at points of strain for added strength, and a zipper fly. They're ACID-PROOF too! (Medium weight cotton twill trousers (Stock No. 643) are also available).
ENDUROWEAVE DACRON/RAYON GABARDINE TROUSERS
STOCK NO. 1643..ONLY $8.25

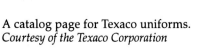

A catalog page for Texaco uniforms.
Courtesy of the Texaco Corporation

A view of very popular collectibles, the famous 1920s and 1930s style green oil containers. Note the outstanding 2 quart pouring can.

Not often found are home lubricant cans like this one.

A close-up of the famous two-quart pouring can, a necessity carried by motorists of the 20s and 30s.

Another motoring necessary was the water pump grease carried in this can.

A two-pound can of chassis lubricant, c. 1920s.

A 1930s bulk oil can.

A nice example of a 1930s motor oil can with a spout that serves as a carrying handle.

Late 20s, early 30s oil can with swivel spout.

Texaco 574 Oil can, the most commonly found of the green label oil cans.

Early Texaco Spica oil can, the one pint size.

1920s Texaco 25 lb. cube can of Thuban S compound.

On the left, an early unidentified can from the Texas Company facility at Port Arthur, Texas. To the right, a 1920s era pint size green label Spica oil can.

Illustration of a Denver-type service station, Tulsa, Oklahoma, c. 1930.
Courtesy of the Texaco Corporation

1950s style Texaco station, showing pump style and arrangement of other equipment.

A universal 5 gallon gas can from the 1920-1930s era.

A "Havoline" embossed one quart oil container, screw-top style.

A one quart screw-top oil container, with a Texaco label inserted to show origin.

From Houston, Texas, an example of a city-type Texaco service station, c. 1930.
Courtesy of the Texaco Corporation

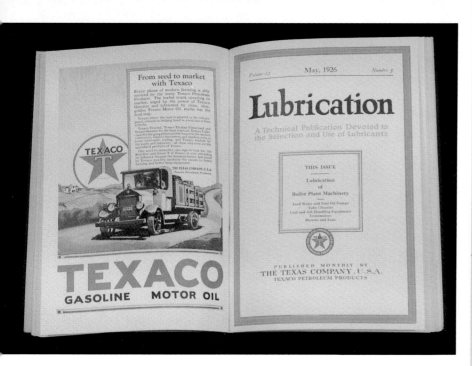

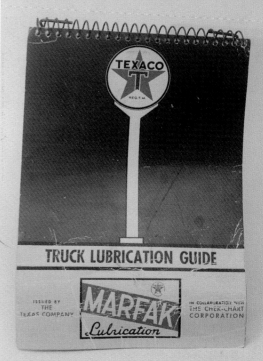

A collector's find! A hardcover copy of the Texaco lubrication manual published from the 1920s through the 1950s, with many interesting pictures throughout the book.

Another paper collectible from the 1950s is the 12.0" x 18.0" Gas Station lubrication guide

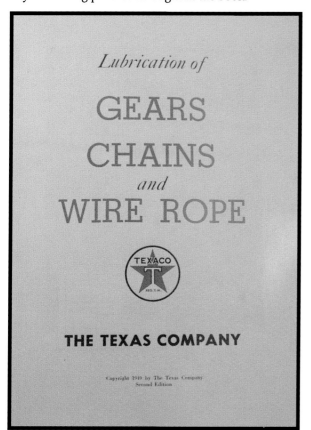

An unusual acquisition is this 50-pound cardboard container of railroad grease. This is considered a rarity because of the packaging material involved.

An interesting addition to a collector's selection of manuals is this booklet on lubrication of gears, chains and wire ropes from 1949.

Assorted products in steel cans distributed by Texaco gas stations during the 1960-1970s; on the left and right are two different styles of radiator flush cans, while Fuel System Conditioner and De-Icer and Super Motor Detergent occupy the middle.

A view over the years. From left to right: a 1960s Texaco style can; a 1950s Texaco Caltex style container can, and lastly, a 1930s Marfak No. 3 can.

A 1960s era Marfak grease can, utilizing the horizontally contrasting colors to offset the product.

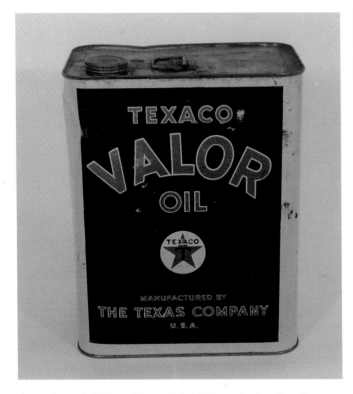

An early style Valor oil can with folding wire handle, circa 1940s.

A later variation of the Valor oil can. Note the change in the carrying handle to a rigid form, as well as the change in lettering on the can.

A grouping of assorted style and size oil cans by Texaco.

It almost appears as though recycling was practiced in 1935! This picture gives a good close view of a Denver-type Texaco service station of that period. Note the tile roof and the rustic bench under the window.
Courtesy of the Texaco Corporation

Chicago, Illinois also shows further evidence of keeping the environment free of the oil can empties. This is a nice example of a Type "E" Texaco service station., c. 1935.
Courtesy of the Texaco Corporation

1950s Caltex and Texaco one gallon Thuban cans.

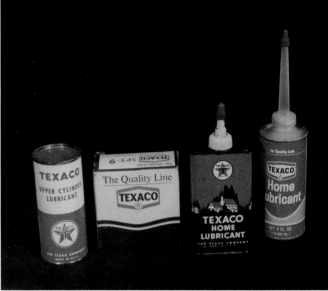

An assortment of Texaco gas station products from the 1940s through the 1970s. From the left, Upper Chassis Lubricant, a carton of SPT 9, and two different varieties of Home Lubricants.

1950s Texaco 5 gallon oil can.

1970s Texaco 5 gallon oil can.

A one pint can of Texaco Super Motor Detergent from the 1960s

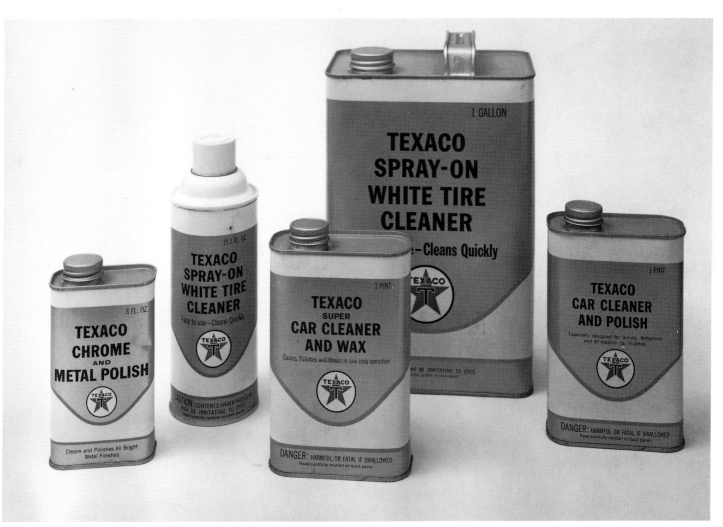

A very small sampling of Texaco products for service station retail sales.
Courtesy of the Texaco Company

An assortment of Texaco and Havoline one quart motor oil cans from the 1950s and 1960s, including aircraft engine oil.

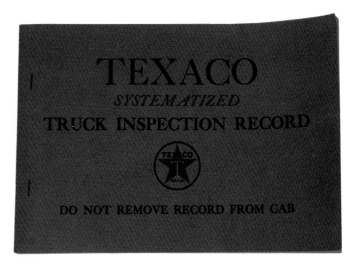

A 1940s systematized Truck Inspection Record Book.

1940s Texaco station road map holder, with period road maps.

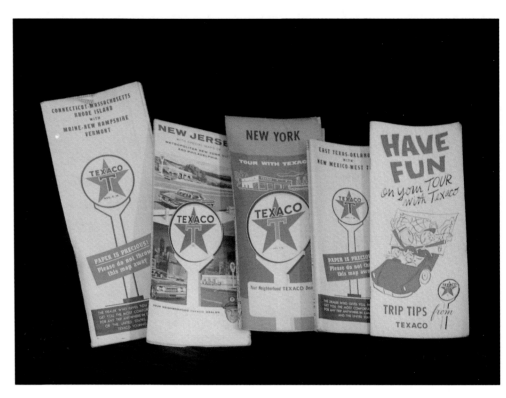

This assortment of road maps are all from the 1960s, in great condition.

Collecting the early road maps can be a fascinating aspect of specialization, as witnessed by these early road maps and cruising charts.

A great find is this early road map in excellent condition. These pieces need not be expensive, and they can often be found at flea markets and swap meets.

During the 1950s, Texaco introduced this box for Regal Starfak No. 2 lubricant.

An unusual find was this sample booklet of asphalt shingle styles for Texaco stations.

A container variant of Texaco Home Lubricant.
Courtesy of the Texaco Corporation

The 1940s saw this can and container for Texaco Home Lubricant come on the market.

This tube of Regal Starfak was marketed in the preceding packaging.

1925 saw the first Denver-type Texaco service station built, as illustrated here.
Courtesy of the Texaco Corporation

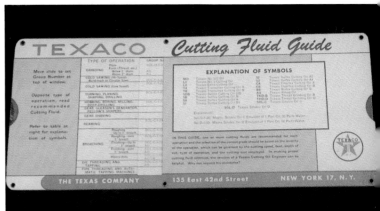

An interesting piece is this Texaco slide rule-type Cutting Fluid guide.

A nice example of a 5 gallon can of Texaco Capella Oil.

A rarity seldom found is this 1930s Texaco salesman's oil and grease sample kit in briefcase format. Notice the various corked grades of oil ranked in holders, while the grease is in fitted containers to the right.

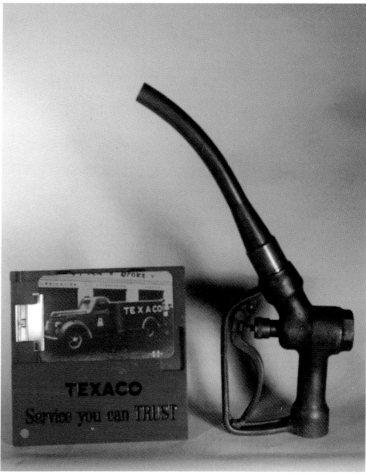

On the left, an early credit card clip board to which is clipped a postcard from the 1940s showing a Texaco tanker, while on the right is a bronze hose nozzle.

An unusual addition to any collection is this Texaco Pilots' Log Book, in green hardcover format from the 1930s.

An assortment of promotional and accessory items found over the years in Texaco stations. From left to right: 1. Texaco salt and pepper shakers from the 1950s; 2. Upper Cylinder Lubricant; 3. Texaco Home Lubricant from the 1940s; 4. A 1990s Texaco dealer's wristwatch; 5. From 1992, Texaco seed packets; 6. (front) A Texaco promotional money clip from the 1940s.

A cap off a 1930s Upper Cylinder Lubricant can.

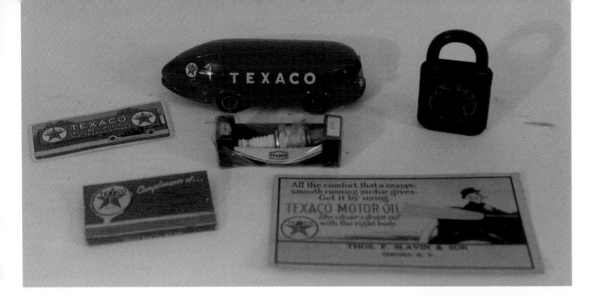

From left to right: Back: a 1920s celluloid fob or key tag; a model of a red Heil Custom Texaco Tanker; a brass padlock with the Texaco logo on the face of the body; Front: a 1950s book of matches; a Texaco-marked sparkplug; and, finally, a 1920s trade card.

From the 1990s, a Burpee package of Starbright Daisy seed as a promotional give-away, courtesy of Texaco.

This Texaco service station in New Orleans, Louisiana, is a wonderful example the "Mission" style service station of the late 1920s.
Courtesy of the Texaco Corporation

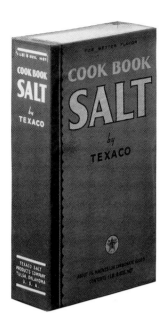

Only on the market for a short period of time, the Texaco salt packages are a collector's coup, if found.
Courtesy of the Texaco Corporation

A 1920-1930s Texaco trade card/blotter, with space for personalization of the station owner.

A rarity from the 1930s: a die-cut bookmark with the Texaco logo and bear cub.

From the Albany, New York area, a 1930s trade card/blotter with the dealer's name, address and phone number.

From Dallas, Texas, a wonderful view of a
1927 Octagon Texaco station.
Courtesy of the Texaco Corporation

Texaco "memo" card, c. 1920-1930.

A grouping from the 1930s
includes a Texaco pot
holder with advertisement,
a dishtowel with the same
message, and, from a time
when fuel gauges were
non-existent, a wooden
gas tank gauge or
measuring stick for a
Model T Ford.

This octagon shaped Texaco station in Houston, Texas, 1929.
Courtesy of the Texaco Corporation

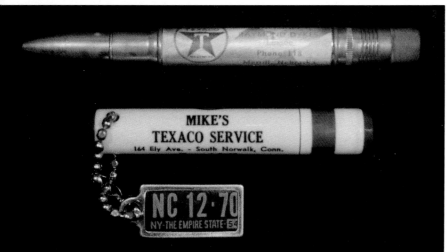

From the 1940s, pencil holders, the bottom one for use as a key chain

A selection of eight different matchbook covers illustrating various Texaco products, all from the 1940s.

More promotional matchbook covers, along with a lighter from the 1940s.

35

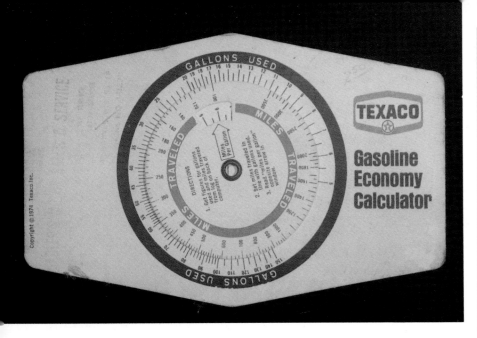

Texaco Gasoline Economy Calculator from the 1950s.

1950s Zippo lighter with Texaco logo.

An assortment of Texaco promotional give-aways, from left to right, top to bottom: 1. A re-useable bottle cap; 2. Golf balls; 3. Zippo cigarette lighter; 4. cuff link; 5. Bic propane lighter; 6. Coffee mug; 7. rare 1960s pint size tin oil can.

Texaco cigarette lighter with 1980s logo.

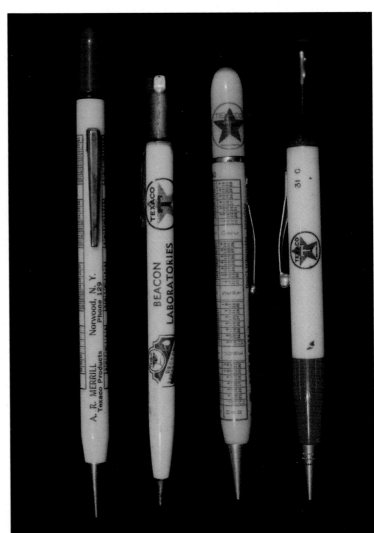

Four Texaco mechanical lead pencils from the 1950s, used for advertising and promotional purposes.

A close-up of the 1940s give-away money clip, with personalized logo.

Dockside give-aways. Texaco playing cards from the 1950s.

Another view of the dockside premium playing cards.

A close-up of the 1940s Texaco key chain.

A hard-to-find Texaco give-away from the 1950s. This is a thermometer in the shape of a Texaco standard, with personalized station information at the bottom.

Another 1950s promotional cookie jar, missing its top. Notice the difference of the additional wording in the logo.

A great promotional item from the 1950s. A Texaco cookie jar with rustic wood handle and top.

Three great collectibles of Texaco, from left to right: 1. A lubrication booklet in the shape of an oil can; 2. Cardboard Texaco eyeshades; 3. Texaco patch for the uniform shirt.

Reverse of the previous Texaco cookie jar.

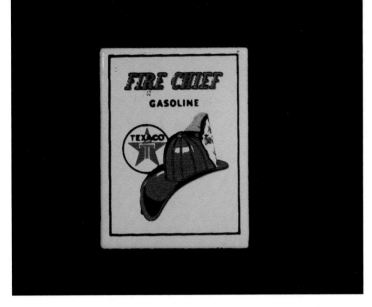

Small, but collectible is this lapel pin with clutch back from the 1950s.

Texaco lapel badge with tie-tack attachment.

Texaco lapel badge with tie-tack attachment.

A plastic frisbee with the current Texaco logo, paired with a Texaco uniform shirt patch.

Marketing tools: a 1950s promotional Texaco ashtray, accompanied by 1970s Rubik-style puzzle cube.

Reusable plastic soda bottle cap from the 1960s.

Promotional give-away golf ball with the 1980s logo.

Another promotional give-away golf ball in orange, with the 1980s logo.

Early 1950s Texaco beverage container

Texaco table lamp in the form of a gas pump globe, for use in the den of a gas memorabilia collector.

1990s styrofoam coffee container.

Fenway Park beverage cup with Texaco logo.

Plastic 1980s coffee cup from "Snappy Jack's" of Mansfield, Texas, a well-known Texas service station, and quite collectible.

1990s glass coffee mug, as sold in Texaco stations.

1970s Texaco old-fashioned glass.

1990s coffee mug from Texaco Food Mart stations.

Exterior view of 1980s Texaco Industrial line give-away, containing a kiln fired personalized tile coaster.

Opened, showing the coaster in its cardboard container.

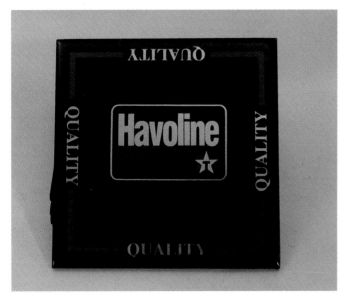

1950s promotional ashtray personalized for a Williamsport, Pennsylvania fuel oil distributor.

Four piece coaster set advertising Havoline motor oil, from the 1980s.

1992 Olympics bumper or windshield sticker by Texaco.

Folder for premium stamps earned by filling up. The affixed stamps earn dollars off your Texaco bill. C. 1993

1980s Texaco give-away plastic litter bag.

Collectible numbered decorator Texaco print from 1982. Great in a den!

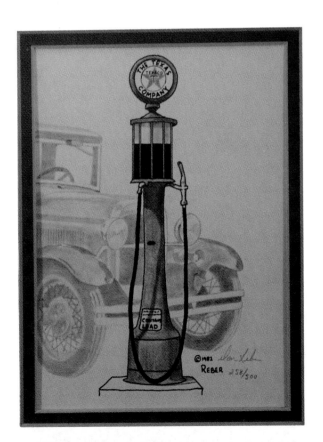

Another un-numbered decorator print from 1982 by Reber.

An early Texaco advertisement, c. 1929-1930s. Note the Zeppelin behind the globe on the Texaco pump.
Courtesy of the Texaco Corporation

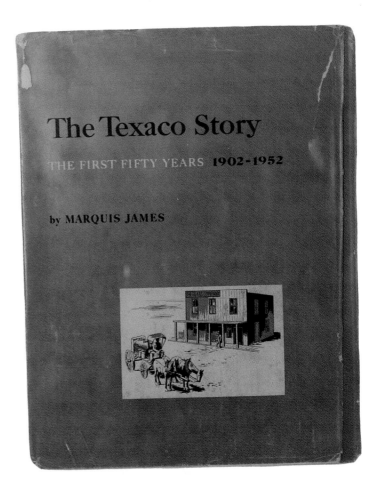

Released in 1952, "The Texaco Story" gives the history of Texaco's first fifty years.

October, 1930 Texaco advertisement from *The Ladies' Home Journal*. At the time, 24% of licensed drivers were women!

Decorator print from the Saturday Evening Post of a 1926 station pump.

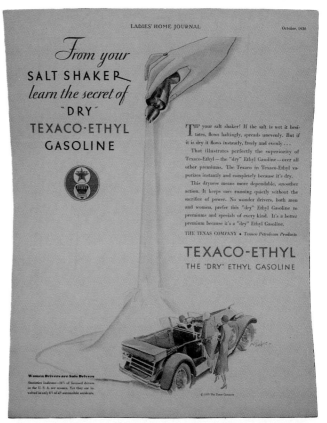

1931 magazine advertisement telling the public that the use of Texaco will hold down the cost of expensive repairs. Note the comparison with the Stratford, Connecticut station shown on the acknowledgements page!

Advertisement from the November 1930 issue of *The Ladies' Home Journal*. As you can tell at first glance, there is a world of difference between advertising then and now!

Texaco magazine advertisement from 1934 featuring Ed Wynn, Texaco's Fire Chief.

1930s post card, featuring Ed Wynn, Texaco's Fire Chief; note the felt Fire Chief's hat.

A Texaco Star Theatre advertisement featuring "Mr. Television"-Milton Berle; c. 1950.
Courtesy of the Texaco Corporation

Over the years, Texaco developed the use of promotional toys to further advertise their products, as seen by this magazine display featuring the Texaco "Buddy L" toy tank truck.

Magazine promotional advertisement for a toy Texaco tank ship. Note that the uniform and cap worn by the model are highly collectible, and command premium figures when found. This model is shown in the Texaco toys section of the book.

Magazine advertisement for a toy scale-model Texaco service station. Check under the Texaco toys section for another view of this model.

A 1950s advertisement in the *Saturday Evening Post*, showing a Texaco standby, the Firehouse Dalmatian pups, advertising Fire Chief gasoline.

More of the Firehouse pups in an advertisement from the *Saturday Evening Post* from the 1950s.

1950s magazine advertisement featuring the Firehouse pups in a familiar scene.

Giant (approximately 2.5' by 3.5') Texaco station poster advertising the Texaco Fire Pumper toy truck. A highly collectible item!

Double page advertisement for a 1960s toy Texaco Fire Pumper. Compared to today, the prices don't look too bad, do they?

Collecting Texaco Signs, Banners and Flags

Some of the earliest signage used by Texaco is depicted on the following pages. Covering a broad spectrum, they include signs used in service stations, on company trucks, on distribution facilities, and even the flags flown at Texaco dock facilities. These signs are now being reproduced, which is unfortunate, as the novice collector must be constantly on guard, lest they be fooled. Some reproductions are clearly marked as such, but there are also many others that deliberately duplicate the original with the clear intent of fooling the buyer. To aid in your search, watch for chipping around screw holes, hair-line age cracks in the porcelain, and rusting spots, which can be helpful in verifying authenticity.

Again, visit your local Texaco station, ask for any Texaco items they may plan to dispose of, or offer to buy them if that's what it takes. What may seem common today is tomorrow's collectible, and it's the wise collector who looks to the future.

Sheet steel sign from the 1920s advertising the famous "Easy Pour" two quart motor oil can.

Curved oval sign from the 1930s from a bulk oil distributor.

1993 Texaco station plastic sign for the 1939 Dodge Airflow Coin Bank. Note how prices have increased over the years!

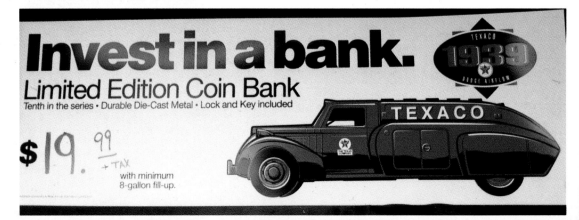

Texaco gasoline pump sign from the 1940s.

From 1933, a truck door sign...hard to find!

1934 Texaco "No Smoking" sign.

An original Texaco "No Smoking" sign dated "6-6-59." Be on
the watch, as these signs are now being reproduced.

A Texaco utility sign from the 1940s for aviation gasoline.

A Texaco trademark utility sign from the 1940s.

1950s pump sign insert.

A marine dockside flag from the 1950s.

Texaco Sky Chief pump sign, circa 1959.

Star from a 1950s Texaco gas station.

Large (approximately 2.5' by 4.5') 1956 Marfak sign from Texaco.

1959 Dockside "Sky Chief Marine" gasoline pump sign.

Texaco uniform patches from the 1950s and 1960s.

1959 Texaco gas pump sign.

1960 Diesel Fuel pump sign.

Vinyl 1970s pump decal.

1980s Texaco station flag.

Texaco gas station sign.

Stained glass leaded Texaco sign for corporate-designed gas station.

Current Texaco oil rack insert.

Texaco license plate emblem shown mounted.

53

An example of a reproduced "kerosine" sign for collectors.

An original rest room sign and keyholder.

Another example of a reproduction collectors sign; collectors should constantly be alert to these being passed off as originals.

A nice example of a 1960s Texaco pocket patch.

Current vinyl Texaco replacement decals.

Texaco Toys

In no other way can a business capture the heart of a future market base than by utilizing the appeal of their own line of toys, or toys featuring their own distinctive logo. Over the years, Texaco, in its wisdom, has offered a vast array of Company toys, from trucks, cars, vans, fleet tankers to airplanes, all covering the spectrum of the Company's long history.

Companies such as Marx, Keystone, Wyandotte, Chein, Gibbs, Tootsietoy and Matchbox, as well as many other famous and not-so-well-known toy manufacturers were quick to get on board, producing their own versions of Texaco's equipment. Included in this rush to the toy market were the gas stations of yesterday, the roadside stands, different styles of gas pumps and auxiliary equipment, model station attendants...in fact, just about anything that would entrance a child, or a grown-up with memories of their own childhood.

Made of slush castings, pressed steel, and pressed tin, most toys were to be found on the counters of the local 5 and 10 cent store, at prices ranging from 5 cents to 25 cents. Common in their time, they are now avidly sought by toy collectors, as well as those collectors specializing in the wares of a particular company, such as Texaco. Toys made by "Buddy L" were higher on the price scale, being larger and made of pressed steel. They were able to hold up under rough and tumble play much better than tin toys, or those made of slush metal.

The toys manufactured for Texaco are marvels of quality production, being accurate down to the smallest detail, regardless of the scale. These toys, while mass produced, are fine examples of the toymaker's art. On the following pages are most if not all of the toys in the Texaco toy line, the fruits of one persistent collector's labors.

Marx automotive toys were popular for decades with children and collectors alike. This is an outstanding example of a 1920s service station.

A 1930s Marx gas pump island.

A beautiful Gibbs 1920s wood and tin Texaco service station.

Keystone composition board Texaco gas station from 1938 set up as a Christmas scene.

ENGINEERS BUILDERS
THE AUSTIN METHOD
2-12-35   Serial 3959-3
Texas Distributing Co.,
Cleveland, Ohio
Porcelain Enamel Serv.Sta.14x18

Cleveland, Ohio, showing the type "E" Texaco service station of porcelain enamel; many toy stations were modeled after this particular style.
Courtesy of the Texaco Corporation

Marx 1939 Sunnyside service station with twin pumps.

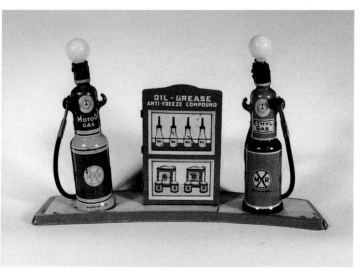

Marx 1938 twin pump service island.

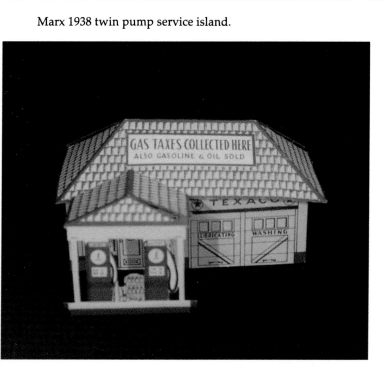

Marx twin gas pump island from the 1940s.

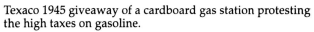

Texaco 1945 giveaway of a cardboard gas station protesting the high taxes on gasoline.

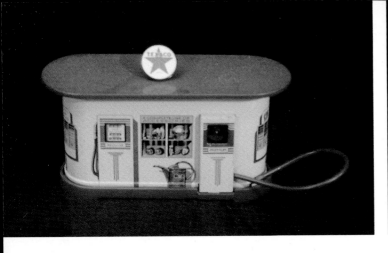

German-made race track (slot car) Texaco station.

Texaco service station and tank truck from an H.O. gauge train set.

Tin litho Texaco service station.

Current manufacture tin litho box representing a 1950s Texaco service station.

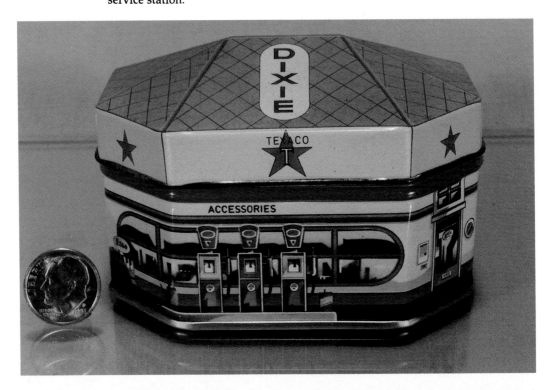

A Texaco service station, Type "EM" from somewhere in the
Mid West Region, c. 1950.
Courtesy of the Texaco Corporation

This plastic Texaco refreshment stand was
made for a railroad layout.

Match Box pressed tin garage and
service station from the 1960s.

Typical of the 1950s is this Texaco Type "EM" service station.
Courtesy of the Texaco Corporation

1960s pressed tin litho Texaco service station, as advertised by
the company.

From the 1970s, a Texaco pressed tin litho gas station with vehicles.

This plastic and tin pump station was made for a German railroad layout.

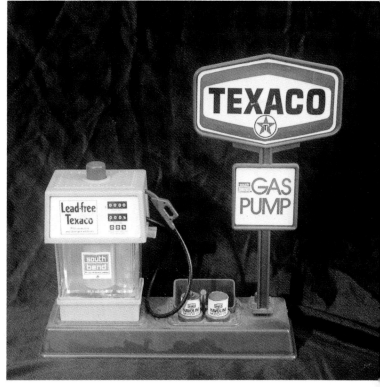

Manufactured by South Bend, this Texaco gas pump island and equipment is made of plastic.

You would have noticed this Texaco service station at Virginia
Ave. and E St., N.W., Washington D.C., in 1956.
Courtesy of the Texaco Corporation

This pressed tin Texaco gas station from the 1950 is typical of
the period. Note the Texaco trucks.

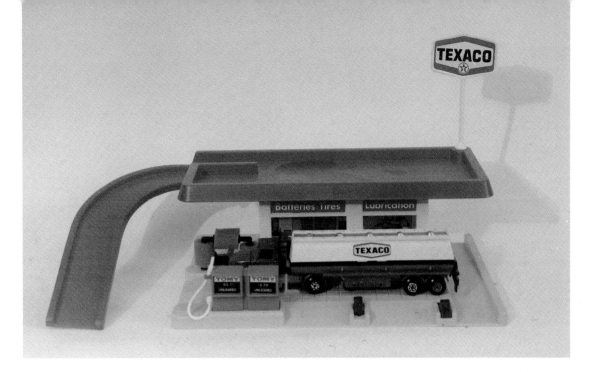

A view of the future for gas stations, in plastic, with a Texaco tanker by "Buddy L" in front of the station. The drive-on roof top parking area never seemed to catch on, other than with toys.

Driving through Springfield, Massachusetts in 1958, you might have come across this Type "EP" Texaco service station.
Courtesy of the Texaco Corporation

This is another example of the Texaco Type "EP" service
station, c. 1950s.
Courtesy of the Texaco Corporation

North Miami, Florida was the location of this PMMA proto-
type Texaco service station, c. 1965.
Courtesy of the Texaco Corporation

At the left is a plastic H-O gauge layout of a Texaco pump station. To the right is a 1930s Texaco toy train tank car.

Oil rig for a toy train layout. Note that the derrick and the cricket would not be at the same location.

Model of a 1940s style Texaco railroad tank car, made in Germany. 18.0" long.

Texaco pumping station for a model railroad layout. Approximately 14.0" long.

Wood and plastic Texaco toy railroad tank cars from the
1950s.

A fine pair of pre-World War II toy railroad Texaco tank cars.

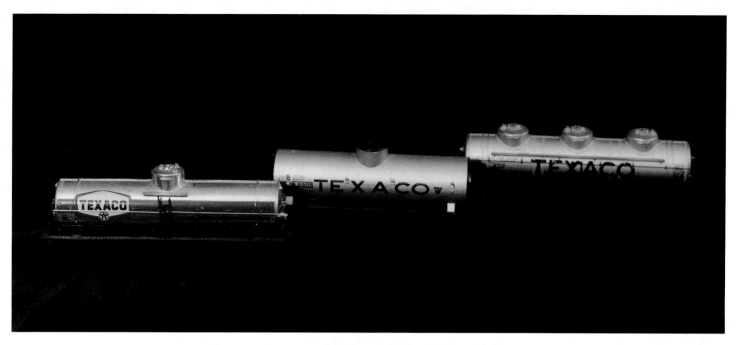

Three excellent examples of model railroad Texaco tank cars of differing designs.

A rare and early unidentified cast iron gas pump, with visible moving indicator on the face of the pump, equipped with a shoelace hose! 6.38" high.

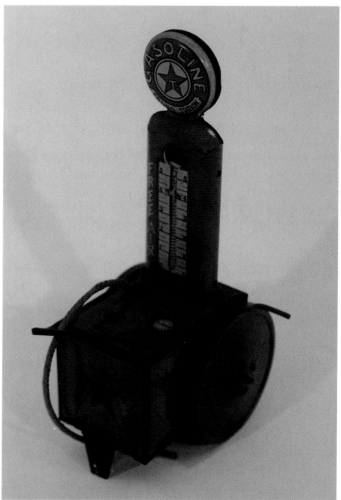

A very rare and collectible tin toy portable gas pump with Texaco markings, by J. Chein & Co., circa early 1930s.

A rare Arcade-made cast iron gas pump from the 1930s, 6.25" high.

From left to right, a toy visible gas pump by Rich Toy Co.; a lovely 1950 plastic bank model of a pump; and a 1980s model of a visible gravity pump.

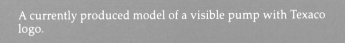

A currently produced model of a visible pump with Texaco logo.

A beautifully done ceramic texaco pump from the 1950s.

Another currently produced model of a visible pump, with a body different than that at the bottom of page 68.

Heavy die cast toy gas pump, circa 1960s. The manufacturer is unknown.

From the 1970s, a "Buddy L" toy gas pump.

Quite rare and collectible is the child's toy storage chest in the form of a Texaco gas pump. The back is open, with shelves for toys. 40.0" high by 20.0" wide.

One of the ultimates in Texaco collecting! A telephone made in the shape of a Texaco gas pump! Just what every den needs.

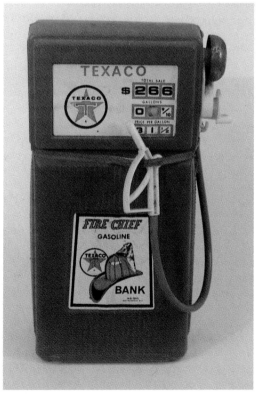

From the 1960s, a child's toy Texaco gas pump.

Early "Ed Wynn" felt Fire Chief's hat, long a popular offering for children by Texaco during the 1930s.

A later version of the Fire Chief's hat made from pressed fibre.

From the 1960s, a toy Fire Chief's helmet with siren, an updated promotional version by Texaco based on the old Ed Wynn helmet.

Another plastic-coated version of the Fire Chief's helmet from the 1960s.

Texaco ventured into the field of trading cards with this set of
the Texaco Star Team.

In 1983, Texaco came out with their first issue in the Texaco
promotional bank series. Number 1, the 1913 Model T Van, is
a very rare and difficult-to-find classic.

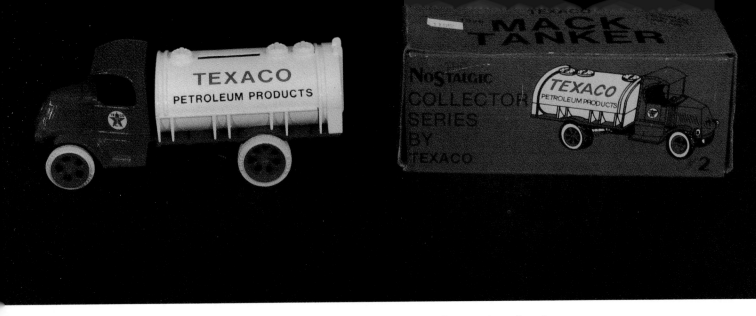

Number 2 in the Texaco promotional bank series, introduced
in 1985, was the 1925 Mack tanker truck.

1986 saw the introduction of the 1932 Ford Delivery Van,
Number 3 in the Texaco promotional bank series.

Number 4 in the Texaco promotional bank series was the 1905 Ford Van, brought out in 1987.

The 1918 Ford Runabout was the 1988 entry in the Texaco promotional bank series, which made it number 5 in the series.

Number 6 in the Texaco promotional bank series was the 1932 Ford Van.

1990 was the year Texaco introduced Number 7 in the series of promotional banks, the 1930 Diamond Tank Truck.

An excellent photo of a vintage 1930s tank truck showing the Texaco name and door sign.

One of the less popular of the series of Texaco promotional banks was Number 8, the horse-drawn tanker brought out in 1991.

Number 9 in the Texaco promotional bank series was the 1925
Kenworth stake truck, introduced to the public in 1992.

Latest in the series of promotional banks is Number 10, the
1939 Dodge Airflow tanker truck, introduced in 1993.

Two models of Texaco-sponsored racing cars next to a can of
Texaco motor oil. Note the early version of Number 5 with the
six-sided logo.

Four assorted toy tank trucks, based on Texaco custom tankers, slush and diecast, from the 1930s to the 1950s.

Unidentified pot metal toy tank truck with rubber wheels from the 1940s and 1950s, representative of a Texaco tank truck.

Three toy trucks: left, an early Match Box Mack Tanker truck; center, a die cast tank truck from the 1950s; right, a Japanese-made tin friction truck from the 1950s.

A Hubley Kiddy Toy Streamline Tanker, representing a copy of the Dodge 1938 Texaco Airflow Tanker; circa 1940s.

A glimpse of the future! A Heil Custom Texaco Tanker from the 1930s.

A late-1930s Texaco tanker manufactured by Tootsie Toy.

Slush cast Texaco toy tank truck, 1950s.

A die cast Texaco marked tank truck from the 1950s.

A beautiful early Texaco open body truck with hand-made products drums. Note the shovel on the running board. 16.25" in length.

A great plastic model of a Mack Bulldog chain drive Texaco tank truck, circa 1920s. Length 14.38".

Early cast iron Texas Company fuel truck. 12.50" long.

Left, a Tootsie Toy early Texaco tank truck, 3.0" long; right, a Japanese-made tin friction Texaco tank truck; 9.75" long.

A close-up view of the Tootsie Toy Texaco tank truck in the previous photo.

A Havoline coin bank with, to the right, a Japanese-made
Texaco tin friction truck. 6.50" long.

From the 1960s, a Japanese-made tin friction truck with
Texaco markings. Length 12.0"

Solido scale model small Texaco delivery truck, vintage 1950s.
3.25" long.

Beautifully executed model of a 1930s Texaco Delivery Truck, made in the 1980s. 6.0" long.

Modeler's alteration of a chain drive Army truck to a gasoline tanker, done during the early 1940s. length 9.38".

From the 1950s, a "Buddy L" promotional toy Texaco Tanker Truck.

Introduced in 1970 by Texaco, a Texaco Jet Fuel Airport Tank Truck.

1950s Gas station wrecker with Texaco markings. This resembles the "Buddy L" tanker in basic design.

Eligor Models, made in France, showing from the left, a Texaco Ford wrecker; a Texaco Ford Tanker; a Texaco Ford Pick-up truck. These models are currently being manufactured.

Texaco marked "Buddy L" van. Note that the red roof light is missing.

Another view of the previous Texaco "Buddy L" van, with the side doors open to show the products drum.

Current manufacture Match Box King model of a Texaco Tank Truck.

Texaco Promotional Christmas Toy Fire Pumper, a great collectors item when all extra equipment is present.

"Days Gone" Model 1942 Dodge 4x4 Van, with Texaco markings; made in England in the 1990s.

A toy Texaco tank truck by "Buddy L."

A plastic model of a Texaco Tank Trailer from the 1960s. 18.0"
in length.

A "Man" Texaco tanker truck made in Germany during the
1960s.

1970s model of a Texaco tank truck.

1980s French-made Ford Tank Truck with Texaco markings.
This is a hot-wheels type model.

From 1983, the Texaco "Indy 500" Team Truck.

A 1980s Texaco toy promotional tanker.

Super King Match Box Gas Station Transporter Truck,
German-made from the 1980s.

1990s Promotional Texaco Tanker Truck.

Early 1990s plastic Texaco race car. Note the black background Texaco logo.

Large plastic model of Texaco race car Number 7 with the six-sided Texaco logo. 18.0" in length.

From the 1980s, a large (18.0" long) Texaco Team racing car.

Collectible stock car model and trade card from the 1990s of
Davey Allison, whose life tragically ended in the summer of
1993.

Promotional bank by Texaco of the Texaco racing car; this
item was pulled from the shelves of Texaco stations after
Allison's untimely death.

The Texaco Racing Team Truck of the late Davey Allison.

"Buddy L" toy Tank Truck with "Paragon Fuel" markings.
Paragon was owned by Texaco, but was allowed to use the
family name for a limited period of time.

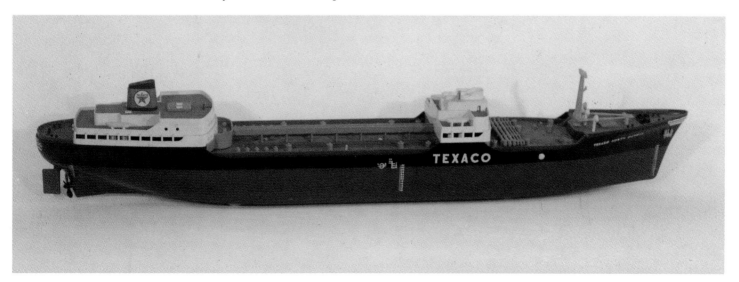

The Texaco Tanker "North Dakota," a promotional toy offered
by the Company.

The S.S.Illinois, a Texaco tanker typical of the tankers used during the first World war. Built in 1913, this picture was taken by a German U-boat officer in 1917 just prior to the ship being torpedoed.
Courtesy of the Texaco Corporation

Laid down in 1972, the "Texaco Amsterdam" is representative of the tankers that ply the seas carrying Texaco fuel oils around the world.
Courtesy of the Texaco Corporation

The Texaco tanker "Africa" on sea trials during 1974.
Courtesy of the Texaco Corporation

The Texaco name carried amidships on the "Africa."
Courtesy of the Texaco Corporation

The funnel of the "Africa."
Courtesy of the Texaco Corporation

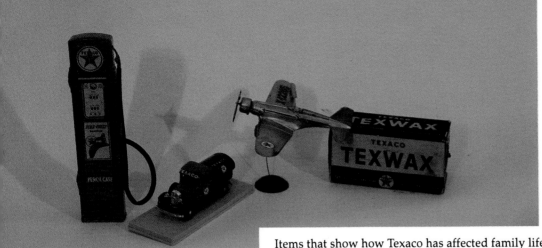

Items that show how Texaco has affected family life in America. From the left: a pencil case in the shape of a gas station pump, from the 1950s; a French-made model of a fuel delivery truck from the 1940s; a pedestal-mounted model of the Texaco racing plane from the 1930s; Texwax, a paraffin wax developed by Texaco for canning and ironing.

A beautifully preserved early model of a pressed steel high-wing monoplane with Texaco markings, circa 1920-1930s. 28.0" long.

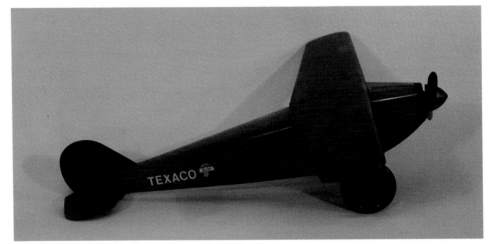

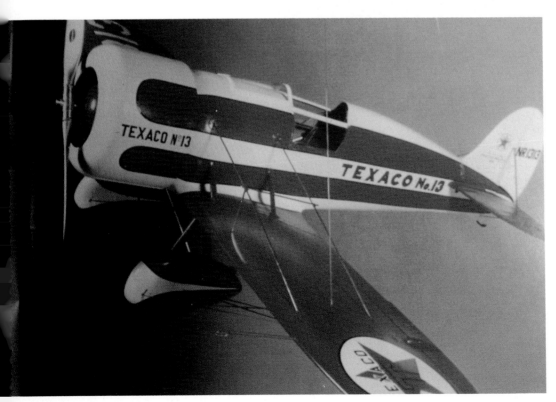

A view of the Texaco Travelair Mystery ship, as presently exhibited in the Smithsonian. *Courtesy of Syl Kill*

The First Edition of "Wings of Texaco," a Texaco promotional toy, 1993.

This interesting model is a "pirate" copy of Texaco Number 13, the Travelair Mystery plane, made in China without permission of Texaco. This was done in 1990.

From the 1930s, this is a wood kit model of the famous Texaco racing plane flown in the U.S. Air Races.

Texaco #1, the Ford Tri-motor that became the first in a long series of aircraft used by Texaco for surveys, regional commuting, business travel and promotional purposes, shown here in logo style. On the following pages will be found most, but not all of the planes used by Texaco well into the 1940s. Unfortunately, pictures of some of the later planes have not survived.
Courtesy of the Texaco Corporation

A great picture of Texaco #1 undergoing an engine checkup. This plane was placed in service in 1928.
Courtesy of the Texaco Corporation

Cast iron toy gas truck with rubber tires from the 1930s. Unmarked, 3.50" long.

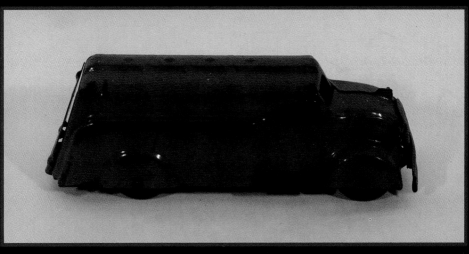

Stamped steel gas truck in the shape of the Texaco Dodge Airflow of 1938. Unmarked, 9.0" long.

Hubley Model A kit car of metal construction; ideal for a 1930s Texaco station setting.

Not often found in such good condition is this Auburn racing car made of rubber from the 1930s. It would be a great accent for a Texaco station.

A professionally restored 1930s Metal Craft truck in "Pure Oil" logos and wording; accompanied by two different styles of early gas pumps.

From the 1930s, this "Buddy L" tank truck is 24.0" long.

In wonderful, un-restored condition, this cast iron unidentified gas truck with open cab is from the early 1930s. 5.0" long.

Unidentified slush cast 4 section fuel transporter with rubber wheels. Length is 3.0".

Dinky Toy Meccano Ltd., rubber wheeled toy British tank Truck, c. 1930s. 4.0" long.

Cast iron 4 section tank gas tanker truck, cab and trailer with
steel wheels, made in the 1930s. Manufacturer unknown. 5.50"
long.

English wind-up tin truck with Esso markings, from the
1950s.

Green Tootsie Toy Tank Truck, slush cast with rubber wheels,
c. 1940. 4.25" long.

A very interesting and desirable collectible from the 1940s is this articulated tin tank truck by Mettoy, made in England. During and immediately after World War II, all oil and gas supplies were "pooled" throughout England, with the tanker trucks being so labeled, and the vehicles themselves painted a rather nondescript gray/blue shade. Length 7.87".

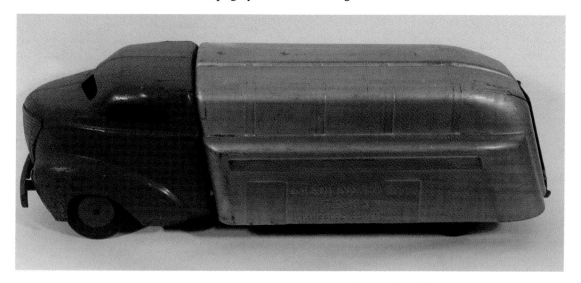

An all-steel and aluminum Wyandotte gasoline tank truck, c. 1950s. 24.0" long.

One of the many promotional trucks put on the market by Hess Gasoline.

Corgi Major Toys 1960s gas tanker, 2.05" in length.

Articulated tanker truck with Mobil markings, by an unidentified maker, c. 1960s. Length is 6.0".

Lesney-made Thorneycroft articulated tractor and 2400 gallon trailer tanker, made in England for Mobil, c. 1975. 4.0" in length.

"Fred Green Toys" articulated tanker/transporter, slush cast with rubber wheels, c. 1970. 6.0" long.

Tootsie Toy slush cast fuel tank truck with plastic wheels, c. 1970s. Length is 2.50".

Japanese-made pressed tin gas truck, c. 1970-1980s. 11.0" long.

Lesney of England-made toy fuel transporter with metal wheels, c. 1980s. 2.0" long.

Currently imported from mainland China for the French toy market is this colorful tin oil tanker.

From the 1920s, we have this rare Marx service station accessory, a portable oil pump in original condition.

"Toytown" 8.0" high tin gas pump from the 1930s.

From Avon Products comes this representative gas pump of the 1920s, filled not with gas, but perfume!

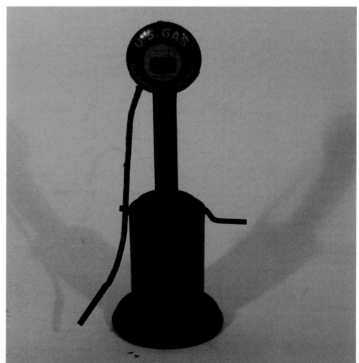

"Toytown" tin gas pump from the 1930s. 12.0" high.

Most unusual is this cardboard gas pump made in Japan approximately 1938.

Sinclair gas pump bank, made from pressed tin, c. 1980s. 4.0" high.

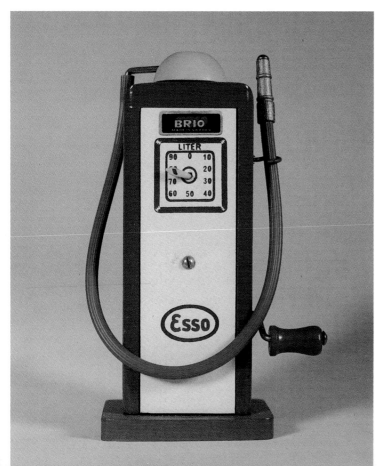

Swedish-made "Brio" toy gas pump, all wood excluding the hose and metal nozzle, c. 1980s. Height 6.0".

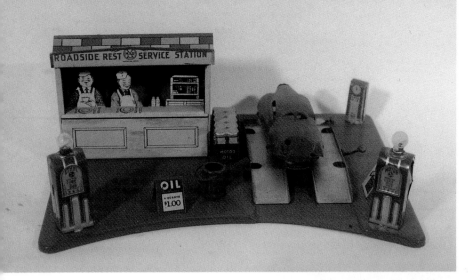

A famous old-timer! The Roadside Service Station by Marx, pressed lithographed tin, c. 1930.

This Wyandotte pressed tin lithographed garage/service station from the 1930s is another familiar old-timer to anyone brought up during that period. Available from the local 5 & 10 cent store for about twenty-five cents, almost every kid in the neighborhood had one! The scene is complemented by the Tootsie Toy tank truck.

In 1939, Marx came out with this "Gull" service station with full apron and hydraulic lift, now a sought-after collectible.

Cardboard Shell gas station by "Built Rite"; from the 1940s. A war-time expedient!

A Japanese-made pressed tin gas station bank and lollypop holder (note holes in the roof for lollypop sticks!), with two tank trucks for accents.

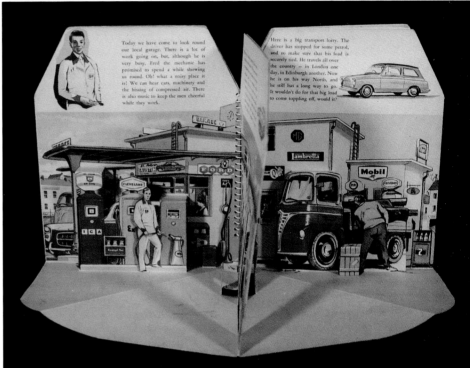

This English pop-up book featuring garage and service station layouts is most interesting and unusual. From the 1960s.

English-made lithographed tin container with car cleaning materials inside.

Unidentified pressed tin gas station and racer, c. 1960s. 1.75" long.

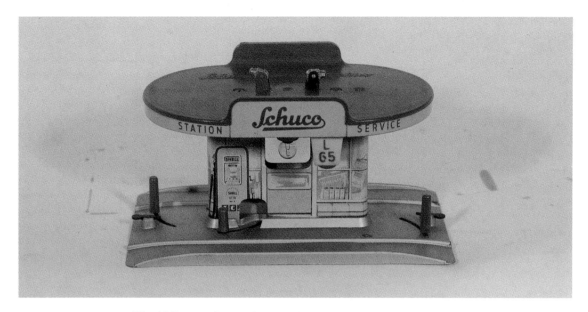

The 1960s saw the production of this German-made "Schuco" slot car set service station.

British-made china "Whimsey Service Station and Garage," hand-painted , c. 1980. 1.50" high by 1.50" long.

Modern Petrol Station gas island, made in England.

TEXACO STAR

March 1916 cover from the Texaco Star.
Courtesy of the Texaco Corporation

Price Guide

Values vary immensely according to the condition of the piece, the location of the market, and the overall quality of the individual item. All of these factors make it impossible to create an accurate value listing, but we can offer a guide. These values reflect what one could realistically expect to pay at retail or auction. It is, however, only a guide, and the author accepts no responsibility for any gain or loss the reader may experience as a result of using this guide.

The lefthand number is the **page** number. The letters following it indicate the **position** of the photograph on the page: T=top, L=left, TL= top left, TR=top right, C=center, CL=center left, CR=center right, R=right, B=bottom, BL=bottom left, BR=bottom right. In photos where more than one object are identified, the values follow the order in the caption. The right hand nimbers are the estimated **values** according to the following chart.

A - up to $50		E - $500 - $750	
B - $50 - $100		F - $750 - $1000	
C - $100 - $250		G - $1000 - $2500	
D - $250 - $500		H - $2500 - $5000	

Page   *Position*   *Value*

Page	Position	Value		Page	Position	Value		Page	Position	Value
8	CL	H		27	BR	A		37	C	A
8	BR	C		28	TL	A		37	BR	B
11	BL	G		28	TR	A,A,A,A,A		38	TL	C
12	TL	G		28	BL	A,A,A		38	TR	B
12	TR	G		28	BR	B		38	B	A,A,A
13	TL	F		29	TC	B		39	TL	A
13	TR	F		29	TR	A		39	TR	A,A,
13	BR	E		29	L	A		39	CL	A
14	TR	C		29	BC	A		39	CR	A,B
14	CR	C,C		29	BR	A		39	BL	A
17	T	A		30	CR	A		40	TL	A
20	TL	B		30	BL	B		40	CL	A
20	TR	B		30	BR	E		40	C	A
20	BL	B		31	TL	B		40	CR	A
20	BR	C,B		31	TR	A,C		40	BL	C
21	BL	D		31	BL	A		40	BR	A
22	TL	A		31	BR	A,A,A,A,A,A		41	TL	A
22	TR	A		32	TL	A,A,C,A,A,A		41	CL	A
23	TL	A		32	CR	A		41	CR	B
23	TR	A		33	CL	C		41	BL	A
23	CL	A		33	CR	A		41	BR	A
23	CR	C		33	BR	A		42	TL	A
23	BR	A,A,A,A		34	C	A		42	CL	A
24	TL	A,A,B		34	BL	A,C,B		42	CR	A
24	TR	A		35	CL	A,A		42	BR	A
24	CL	B		35	CR	A,A,A,A,A,A,A,A		43	TL	A
24	CR	A		35	B	A,A,A,A,A		43	TR	A
24	BR	A,A,A		36	TL	A		43	BL	C
26	TL	B,B		36	TR	A,A,A,B,A,A,A,A		43	BR	C
26	TR	A,A,A,A		36	CL	B		44	TR	A
26	CL	B		36	C	A		44	BL	A
26	CR	A		36	BR	A,A,A,A		44	BR	A
26	B	A		37	TL	B		45	TL	A
27	BL	A,A,A,A,A,A		37	TR	B		45	TR	A

45	BL	B		65	B	B		91	B	A
45	BR	A		66	T	A,A		92	TL	B
46	TR	A		66	B	B,B		92	BR	B
46	BL	A		67	T	A,A,A		93	T	B
46	BR	A		67	BL	C		93	C	C
47	TL	A		67	BR	D		93	B	C
47	TC	A		70	TL	C		96	TL	A,A,A,A
47	TR	A		70	BR	E		96	CR	E
47	BL	A		71	T	C		97	TL	A
47	BR	A		71	BL	B		97	C	D
48	TR	C		71	BR	B		97	B	B
48	CL	D		72	TL	A		110	CL	B
48	BR	A		72	CL	A		110	R	C
49	TL	D		72	BR	A		110	BL	A,A,A
49	TR	B		73	T	A		111	TL	A
49	C	B		73	B	D		111	TR	A
49	B	B		74	T	D		111	C	A
50	TL	D		74	B	D		111	B	B
50	TR	D		75	T	B		112	B	B
50	C	C		75	C	B		112	C	A
50	BR	D		75	B	D		112	B	D
51	TL	C		76	T	A		113	T	A
51	TR	B		76	B	A		113	C	B
51	CL	C		77	T	B		113	B	A
51	BR	C		77	C	B		114	T	A
52	TL	C		77	B	A,A,A		114	C	C
52	TR	A,A		78	T	A,A,A,A		114	B	D
52	CR	A		78	C	A		115	T	C
52	BL	C		78	B	A,A,A		115	C	A
52	BR	B		79	T	A		115	B	A
53	TL	B		80	TR	A		116	T	B
53	TR	G		80	CL	A		116	C	A
53	C	A		80	BR	A		116	B	A
53	B	A		81	T	C		117	T	D
54	TL	A		81	B	B		117	C	B
54	TR	B,A		82	T	B		117	B	B
54	CL	A		82	CR	A,B		118	T	A
54	CR	A		82	BL	A		118	C	B
54	BL	A,A,A		83	T	A,A		118	B	B
55	TR	D		83	CR	B		119	TL	B
55	CR	D		83	BL	A		119	CR	B
55	BL	E		84	T	B		119	CL	B
56	T	D		84	CL	B		119	BR	A
57	TR	D		84	BR	B		120	TL	B
57	CL	C		85	TR	B		120	TR	C
57	CR	C		85	CL	B		120	BL	B
57	BL	D		85	B	A,A,A		120	BR	B
58	TL	A		86	T	B		121	TL	B
58	TR	A,B		87	T	A		121	TR	B
58	CL	B		87	C	C		121	BL	A
58	B	A		87	B	B		121	BR	A
59	CR	A		88	T	B		122	TL	C
59	BL	A		88	C	B		122	CR	A
60	B	C		88	B	B		122	CL	C
61	T	C		89	T	B		122	BR	B
61	CL	C		89	C	A		123	TL	A,B,A
61	BR	B		89	B	B		123	CR	A
62	B	C		90	T	B		123	CL	A
63	T	C		90	C	B		123	BR	A
65	TL	A,B		90	B	A		124	T	A
65	TR	B		91	T	A		124	C	A
65	C	A		91	C	A		124	B	A